G000253432

single window

single window

Daniel Sluman

Nine
Arches
Press

single window

Daniel Sluman

ISBN: 978-1-913437-23-7
eISBN: 978-1-913437-24-4

Copyright © Daniel Sluman, 2021.
All photographs © Daniel Brenchi-Sluman and Emily Brenchi-Sluman, 2021 and published with full permission and consent.
All photographic and image rights reserved.
Cover artwork concept © Daniel Sluman. Layout: Jane Commane.

All rights reserved. No part of this work may be reproduced, stored or transmitted in any form or by any means, graphic, electronic, recorded or mechanical, without the prior written permission of the publisher.

Daniel Sluman has asserted his right under Section 77 of the Copyright, Designs and Patents Act 1988 to be identified as the author of this work.

First published September 2021 by:

Nine Arches Press
Unit 14, Sir Frank Whittle Business Centre,
Great Central Way, Rugby.
CV21 3XH
United Kingdom

www.ninearchespress.com

Nine Arches Press is supported using public funding by Arts Council England.

for Emily   always

CONTENTS

autumn

we watch documentaries on mute

from the sofa we've lived in
for the last eight months

the frames crash over us

the colours
the names
the stories rip   & merge

& we don't sleep or we sleep
all day

when we finally pull back the curtain

a slant of rain is leaning
against the road

slick with rotting leaves

autumn smoulders everything
back to its roots

spoils it

to a hazy gauze
of yellows & browns

we count down the seconds
before our pills sing their gospel inside us

we rock in our seats
eyes rolled back

towards the heaven
of improved conditions

all animals must maintain

however small
however distant it becomes

all day we drink tea piled with sugar

& wake in yesterday's clothes
to this piss-bright sunrise

& our daily bread
is to not let ourselves bend

or break

under the weight
of this light

~

already bored of the way
        the rain slicks the window
& whirls of brassy leaves
        rustle through the grass
fatigue stirs through our bones
        anchors us into the stained sheets
& today the world is just one more thing
        floating past the glass

you log onto your phone
        to see how near the clouds are closing
& i flatten my spine into the carpet
        until each vertebra unfurls
like pearls in a necklace
        i turn my hearing inward
try to hear the moment my pulse skips
        when the opiates slip into my heart
to feel the exact moment the weather turns

~

~

half-awake to the noise / of pages flitting
next to you / like a tongue wetting / like a bird
landing / i drink my tea as quietly /
as i can stare / at an invisible spot / beyond
the tv / until my body & mind / finally meet

~

dusk spills through the curtains
      & carves the room out with light

the pan of burnt eggs soaking in the sink

      the stale smell
    of yesterday's weed

huddled in the corner of the room

      the inflammation flickers
      in your joints

     like a wasp fraught
   in the folds of a curtain

a single finger swipes the screen of your phone

     drawing the last two years of our life
      before you   image by image

the sky outside swells like a bruise
    drawn through a poultice

      & you're dug into the duvet
waiting for the codeine to bloom inside you

the pharmacology of love
is guesswork

night follows day here in diminishing returns

& all i want is to keep as much of you
for tomorrow

~

~

christ

to never swallow a pill

to have a body that barely lifts a whisper

to never find yourself alone

watching the first honeyed light of the day run

to dream of a body held together like a cloud

falling into rain   to gently touch the rooftops

of ruined factories a thousand tender places

at once   to have a body not in need of saving

that doesn't click on & off through the night

like this broken fan   the side effects of our drugs

like badly-cut holes leaking light

over the carpet in agony in doubt   christ

to never need to qualify our love

in bed at night   every tomorrow pressing down

firming almost hard enough to touch

~

the first time i drank morphine
a weight slid over my heart

& the whole summer
collapsed under me

my head packed with ice
phone overflowing with garbled texts

& all because of this vertebra

a firecracker in a closed fist
& morphine   the only thing to smoulder it

how all medicine
pulls you away from yourself

just enough to create distance

topless before the fan
in a pool of sweat

dreaming of dusty fields

where the brittle petals of poppies waiver
in the breeze

i scratch myself awake

skin blistered red
my nails at my body like a hand

at my throat

the morphine pulling life from me slow as a splinter
a syringe squeezed

millilitre by millilitre

~

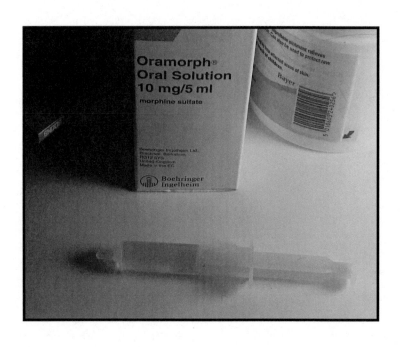

~

the smell of freshly turned earth when we wake

    & the groan of machinery outside
        moving mounds of silt

from one end of the lot to the other

    clearing slabs of chalk
        that jut from the topsoil

        of the town's new rim

      the county-road's rain-filled potholes
      moonlit

& stitching a route
    that we follow in dreams

        as we rustle in our sheets & imagine

        the mound of earth
        in our yard being worked

closer to completion

    as if it were our own child
        moving towards term

at the lip of this bank
a scattering of foxglove sways

in the grip of the october wind

the future tilled frantically
amidst the stink of diesel

& the diggers crude talk & soiled hands

the soles of their steel-capped boots
stretching the world

building on it further around us
without us

~

you say / the way
the sun / catches my hair /
when i'm straddling / your chest /
my belt slipping / through your hands /
is the cleanest want / you've known

~

today
the reasons to live write themselves

the way you fill her hand
at the lightest touch

how i can watch you settle in the mirror
& not be sad or afraid

at these absences that stiffen around you

still   when another autumn morning breathes on the glass
i'll feel the greatest distance between us

my throat
& this voice i stuff down it

you   me   & her

there are times all three of us feel so close
only the barest breeze can slip between us

& there are nights when her smile lifts us
both by the collar

~

winter

a jolt of white against the window
as the snow piles against the glass

& like children
we feel that scattering of flakes outside

melting into the creases
of our open hands

it must have started when we were asleep

like a note drawn from the silence
& trembling louder

with the mounting fall

filling the gutters & packing the furrows
of the road with noise

in the shower the clouds of steam
unfold from my shoulders

like wings

sometimes you telling me
the outline of my hips makes you wet

as i dry myself on the edge of the bed

is all it takes
& i'm suddenly here in my body

my ego in your hands
a pipe splitting in frost

as i fill my form
sudden   maddening as weather

~

~

sprawled back
eyes closed

glasses slide
from my fingertips

& clatter over the edge
of the bed

the body filled
with sleep

slicked with ointment
& slipping through

the mattress
to the bottom

of the sea
a wave crashing

against the screen
of the tv

in one slow furl
of blue

the shadow
of my soft body

cast over the wall
in flashes

half-dreams
piling

like flotsam
against the shore

& how many
of these fish

are now dead
apparitions

glistening
through time

my failing sight
my stack of books

in the near-dark
of the room

a ligament of incense
loosens in the air

the blanket bunched
around my neck

your hand
holding mine

beneath the sheets
the narrator's voice

rises from
the vast bellies

of the whales
themselves

& i can feel
myself turning

into one of these
slow-pulsed creatures

bobbing through
centuries

of sluggish time
with you

the duvet sunk
over me

soft as the jaws
of a basking shark

closing
the shallow pool

of your breath
on my chest

sweetheart
that we might

never label
this feeling

but still swim
towards it

faithfully
each day

~

we light a bowl
& choke on a mouthful of smoke

until the pain in our hips drifts
out the cracked window

through the pipe's blistered glass
the embers burn silver

& we fall asleep listening to music
& reading poems about winter

springsteen whispering
his blue-collar dreams

in our ears

the tongue
of his telecaster stroking our heads

blank

when we smoke too much like this
we come apart in our bodies

the lack of distance

between our actions
& our fantasies giddying

the flare of your hips in half-light
that manic laugh

up close   how your skin shivers

like a line about snow
in a robert frost poem

~

~

like a saint
you kiss the sickliest part of me

eyes shut

the rings slide carefully
from your fingers

until they spill & settle on the table

ponytail drawn
tight against your scalp

your palms oiled

the fine hair on my stump glowing
as you stretch your hands over all this hurt

the stunted hip-bone
& its crest of thickened scar

your knuckles smoothing knots
from the sluggish muscles

that no longer flex the hip
into a half-smile

i imagine the phantom limb

pouring into your palms like water
all the cruel words & shame

thrown into the space
where my leg should be

pulled out like barbs

this is how it feels
to have your trauma held

i tell you your kindness kills me
your grace kills me

your soft lips pressed against this void
kills me again & again

being loved by you
is like turning the volume up so high

you can't hear yourself breathe

~

in an overspilling drawer / of yellowed papers /
on the back / of an old hospital letter /
the odds of my survival / (post-chemo) /
notated as a percentage / (30) / in my father's hand

~

father

i've fallen asleep
at the wheel of my bliss again

head bobbing
over a desk
full of drafts
a swell of crumpled paper cresting
into a wave

scalp caught
in a glittering net of light
from the angle-poise lamp
you rescued from a car-boot
years ago

that now burns a dusty halo
over my shoulders
& makes this the only lit window
on the street
as you drive past
to your early-morning shift

this weekend
you'll help my wife take out the bins
you'll notice the pain
flickering in my eyes

which as a son
is a special kind of failure
        that i should let reality leak
            from my grip

    i'm still writing myself back
            into the corner of the council house
                we lived through
            in the noughties

helping you fold laundry
        in the evening
to make ends meet

            20 years later
        & a road's width
            between your life & mine

        when you've steered
                yourself home
    will you dream of your child's mind
            unpeeling
    against a stiff opiate fog ?

will you drift back to when i was a eleven
        the first time they said
            cancer

how the medication didn't work
& the only solution
was this

strangers
sawing my tiny body open
under a burning plate
of light

~

~

brushing wet hair / and holding
that weighty slap / of dark red
in one hand / to twist into a knot /
& fasten yourself / into sleep

~

                    pans of oil
          cooling through the afternoon

the smell of fried onions drifts
              over our bodies

as we sleep   fully-clothed

          sprawled in a pile   stilled
like marble figures chiselled into the sheets

              necks glazed in sweat

the cards we bought each other greased
          with finger-marks on the table

              & our tiny kitchen stacked with dirty plates

having blistered the red peppers in the oven
              & burnt the garlic into blackened grits

we have pushed our bodies beyond their limit again

                    a chipped coffee cup holding
          hand-picked flowers from the garden

as we spoon through shallow dreams

          skin slippery with smoke & salt
& unable to consummate the ideas in our heads

              having given each other our bodies instead

                    ~

early morning rain / touching
the windows / of different rooms /
in our house / like instruments /
a symphony / opening up
the glass / changes the aspect /
the sound / the weather /
like our moods

~

white sheets contain us in the illusion of containment
  & we don't screw like they do on tv

   the vaseline-smeared lens
  groping bodies that gleam

  the carefully-placed sighs
   & glazed eyes of the beautiful

 swimming through the windows of gyms
  & pools like torchlight

 lonely as hell
they will never love like this

  our whole bodies into the earth
  of each other

we bury ourselves like readers in books
  take each other apart

  & put each other back again & again

  cripples love best
 because love is an assembly

   & we have always been broken

  gluing our lives with glitter & card
  in darkened rooms

~

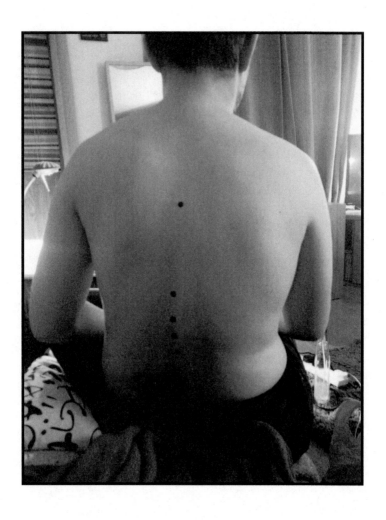

~

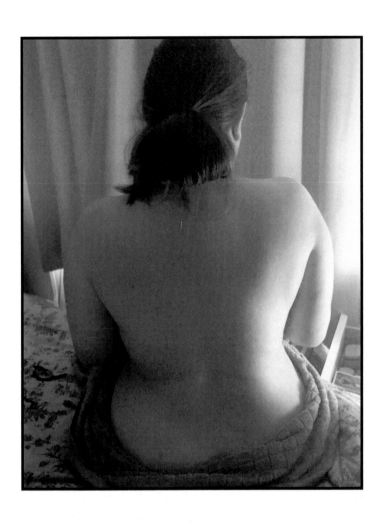

~

spring

your bottom lip sweet with red bull

the pale crease of your collarbone
lengthening in half-light

i pour these memories into paper
as best as i can

& gather you in my arms
to drink each freckle

before we sleep deep in that dark

where my shame sits
in the corner

like my father did
when i was thin as a melon rind with the chemo

learning that the body
is warm milk

& i couldn't sleep
without knowing he was there

just like i can't sleep now

watching my breath shake
each hair

on your neck

~

pain spreads / like piss
pushing through / the creases /
of your jeans / like a moment
remembered / like an idea /
stiffening into clarity

~

one of us is always appearing
to the other

in a scribbled haze of cigarette smoke

used pill-packets spread
like sunlight over the sofa

5mg of diazepam flickering
through my body like rain

in your hand
a bloody scrap of tissue

like a burst party balloon
as you fall asleep on the toilet

the calendar on my phone empties itself

& i tell you it's getting better
but maybe that's just something

people like us say
to stop things falling apart

how we drag ourselves
from week to week

& the world carries the beautiful
like the room carries the light

from the window

~

~

the toilet paper tears in your fist
a curl of blood threads

down the side of the basin

& i can hear your heart straining
from the other side of the door

sat amidst the darkness   & lint

the corpses of spiders stiffened inwards
like tiny fists

& the only light is cast
through the gaps in the doorframe

fine lines of gold   gouged into the floor

as you wait for this flare to blur
you picture the beautiful

all over the world
skin glistening

in the bath as they shave themselves
to a vapour

leafing glossy magazines
& filling prayers

with a thankfulness pitched
against the horror of lives like ours

the skirting boards choked with dust
the late-night tv

preaching its call for wholeness
from the empty lounge

in a minute you'll pull your fingers
from the pockets of your gown

& rest your weight against my arm

& we'll shuffle our way to bed
one step at a time

~

~

a middle-aged woman peels off our socks

& strips us layer by layer
like she's fleecing sheep

the flakes swirl from my shin
the glossy scars on my arms

a reminder
how deep you can cleave the flesh

before the body asks
the blood to swell

of this lapse
between what the body feels

& the mind calls for in turn

she plies our skin
with emollient thick as grease

& we are left to sit in our sweat
like chops spitting in the pan

the quietness that gathers
when she locks the door behind her

& this piece of furniture is all that carries us

adrift
in our pacific-blue hoodies

fingers shaking around our mugs
as the gutters outside choke with ice

& we'll wake tomorrow
in the same bare room

our carer will come again
& again   to unwrap us

until all that's left
are tears

streaming down our necks

onto this sofa
that holds us like a mother

~

some days think i dreamt that journey
but when i close my eyes it's there

the canopy of low-swinging elms
blotting out the sun

& pear-green hedges running
either side of that road

the smell of my father's aftershave gone stale

his loosened tie
& five o'clock shadow

i'm the last child picked up from school

& nothing can crack this quiet joy
held between us

on our way home

the tang of freshly-cut pine
slung on the breeze

& dad's first smoke
of after-work-freedom

flicked

against the rim of the opened window
& into the long grasses

of my memory

~

~

the
width
of
a
pupil
&
gallons
of
light
poured
through
like
cans
of
paint
flooding
the
tiny
aperture
yellows
blues
full-
throated
reds
this
glossy
lens
so
much
presence

so
much
noise
like
being
drowned
in
perfume
like
your
skin
soaked
in
kerosene
&
a
match
lit

~

an oval of grey water laps
around the sides of the tub

& the midday sun peers
through the half-opened window

watching your elbow
dig into my hip in rhythm

with the scraping
of the extractor fan

the droplets of condensation
write & re-write a message

on the wall's peeled paintwork
my fingers slide under

the glittering surface
that premonitory shudder

like the first chords
of a song unravelling   the water

dammed against your hip
the steam gathering between us

like a loom of pale threads
& we could be anyone anywhere

caught in the simplicity
of a spring weekend   pulling the joy

from each other's bodies
in handfuls   the drifts of soap & cum

around us pulling apart
& gently floating together again

~

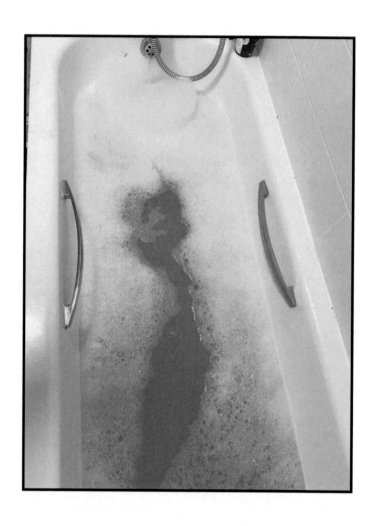

~

the azaleas i bought you
are sweating through their plastic veil

& neither of us can fetch the vase
or trim the stems

the petals gasp against the cellophane

& the canned laughter
from your room reaches me

like the last crackles of light
from some dying star

half-awake
the day washes in & out of the house

i put my earphones in
but music only drags me further from you

dropping emojis & gifs
into each other's phones

the distance between our bodies
always swelling

how a message will hang in the air   unread
& i'll know you've fallen asleep

how i listen out
past the gases sliding in the fridge

& the thud of radiators expanding with heat

until i hear you reach
for your pills & water

& i know i can finally rest   in dreams

we're two sentences on opposing pages
in a cheap book   offset

falling into the heart of the spine
together

~

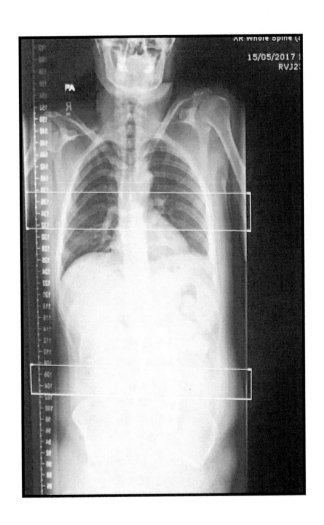

my left-hand suspended
over your chest

the other tracing
the pale monorail of scar tissue

that stretches across your hips

the weather breaking
around the house

clouds bleeding pink
& thunder splitting

over the troposphere

our legs tangled
in a swell of linen

the sliver of moonlight
in the sky

like a needle pressed against cloth

lightning flickering loose
in the distance

as if the world is tearing itself apart
which must be an act of love

(that there is something worth trying for)

we hold this tight
& give ourselves over

to the answers our bodies bring

a gleam of spit catching the light
on your cheek

your ponytail in my fist

the flung stars drifting across the horizon
like trash in a river

~

too much morphine / my face a smear /
in the mirror floating / above the glass /
voice shaking eyes / felt black the bottle /
of blue bleeding out / over the carpet

~

the trousers i will marry you in
spread between your hands
over the living room carpet
needle seized in the corner of your lips
cross-legged & barefoot
you mark with chalk the border
where my body ends
sow the flap of fabric
to tighten the sides into a grimace
& most will never know this intimacy
how you trace every ridge of the lipped pelvis
with the chime of your scissors
making a space in this world for me to fill
rounding the edge to hang off me like a crescent moon
you ply your love seam by seam

~

summer

when i wake

it's with a lit cigarette hung
between my lips

or loose

rolling past startled fingers
into the blanket's folds

this vice of a cough
my plot of careless stars

singed through cotton

these tiny wrecks
in the sheet we shake out in the garden

letting summer pour through
each blunder

every lapse hollowed & held in fabric

another week in this heat
& the junk-mail piles at the door

voicemails gather   spill over
in our phones

& scatterings of ash mark a route to where i lie
on the sofa

my body on fire

~

two paracetamol / a glass of ice-
water / headache clouded / with nausea
unfurling / through the afternoon /
like the resurrection / flower
sucking every drop / of moisture
from my skull

~

~

i float
across the white tiles of the hall

to a hot windowless room
where the nurse bundles the needle in

& the fine nib gathers the blood

from the crook
of my arm

my pulse throbbing behind my eyes
like it did in '98

when i haunted my family for a year
a half-ghost

the tufts of hair falling loose
in my baseball cap

talk of blood counts & chemo
at the dinner table

as we plated slices of meat

now   the woman with the tourniquet
cradles over her concentration

drawing the life
i've rebuilt over twenty years

through her soaped hands

into a glass vial
that warms her fingers

& if she doesn't stop i will die

this desire
to lose a little too much of myself to another

to give what i need most over
is a fantasy i've fallen through

again & again
since the cancer was caught

how the nurse slips the tip
from the pinched skin

& loosens the rubber cord
with a smile

~

~

the long night presses over my hands at the sink
        bowls clatter under water

& the brittle light from the stars
        scorches through the darkness

                a ketchup-smear coagulates
                        & splits off the saucepan

        spiralling
down the drain-hole's milky eye

                when the pain in my sacrum uncoils
                        & stretches

                i surrender rather than fight
                        to slip each sensation

the crickets singing their first song of summer

                until the pain condenses
                        to a bearable thud

the handle of the bread knife turns
        familiar in my palm

                my absent-mind pulling me
        from the darkening whirl of matter in the bowl

                towards the glittering vastness beyond it

~

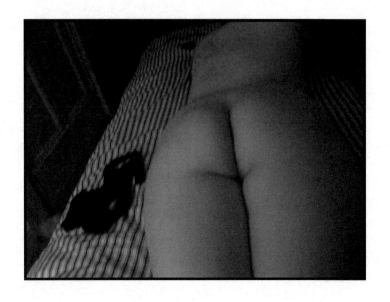

~

flat on my stomach i touch you all over
with my eyes
the butterfly tattoo's silver-blue wings
pinned to your instep
underwear hitched to one side
sometimes   this is more
than watching
more than   anything else
the dark slipping off your limbs
mermaid's love incense stinking up the room
nipples spilt over the top of your bra
& no music except the punch of your breath
& the low stutter
of the vibe
the pale knuckles of one hand cramped
over the headboard
electrical cord snaking between your thighs
& face turning through every shade
of epiphany
the slightly-darker skin of your heels dug
into the bunched sheets
glossy pink varnish chipped
on your toes
when it's over you're swept
like driftwood on the bed
the distance between us
cut

~

                    like a character

about to say something startlingly beautiful
                at the denouement of a film

                        i gather your jaw in my palm

            your hair smells of the apple pancakes
                you fried for us this morning

                        i hold a bowl of tepid water
                            against my thigh

            as you stare at the ceiling
                your head on my lap

                sunlight pouring
        through the pink folds of your ear

                that coil towards
    the chamber of your cranium

        with a cotton bud
    i probe the sides of the aperture

                    peeling the dry skin back
                until the air pops back into your skull

                        whole   like the simplest of ideas

& i nurse you like this three times a day
drawing the infection

away from the drum

with a patience
i could never summon for anyone else

the same way you'll wrap
the gash on my finger next week

each throb of my pulse
soaking the paper a deeper blush of red

my knuckle under the tap
turning the water pink

this subtle insistence
of tending for the other's bodymind

an ideology we uphold
a stitch we pull tight

time & time again

~

your nakedness / settles in the mirror / a hairpin
twisted / between your lips / as you gather / your hair
in a bun / the red slipped between / your fingers
spine arched / painted toes digging / into carpet

~

~

i look back at the street
        & pinch my cigarette
            into the wall
    of this cheap hotel
           the embers fly
        & shepherd's bush trembles
           in the august heat
commuters shouldering
      past each other
          eyes fixed
on the smouldering sidewalk
      as if they could fall
clean through   the pink sky
      pressing itself
over the stained rooftops
      i walk back to our room
& in the biggest city in the world
      you swallow me whole
           we hold each other in bed
      for the first time in weeks
        & kiss
your lips taste of toothpaste
        & the faint sweetness
          of semen
      the value of our bodies
           somehow greater
      wrapped in the sheets

between us

we hold a fortune

spoiling by degrees each day

& here

with the brittlest of my love

in the back of your mouth

the best of me

suspended

somewhere in your dreams

& whatever remains

in your arms

christ

all the great things

we may

or may not do

waiting to be done

& undone

again

Image Descriptions

Unless stated otherwise, images are filtered in cyan blue.

page 16: A darkened view of a rain-flecked window at night from inside the house. There is a vase of flowers on the sill and the glare from two streetlamps is visible through the glass.

page 20: The ceiling of a room at night, including a lampshade and its shadow. The ceiling is lit with stars from an LED Projector.

page 24: On a white bedside table is a prescription bottle of oral morphine solution. In front of it sits a 5ml syringe filled with the solution.

page 35: A shot from inside the house of the same window as on page 16. It is night and snow is piled on the outside windowsill. The light from the streetlamp is caught in the centre of the glass.

page 42: Emily, a young white woman, with long hair and glasses, sits on a sofa with the curtains of the window behind her. She lights a glass pipe with a match.

page 49: An overexposed black and white photograph of the window shown in page 16 and page 35. Light bursts through the window, blurring the edges between the window and the curtains.

page 54: A picture of Daniel's back as he sits on the sofa. Black dot stickers are placed on his spine to follow the curvature of his vertebrae. His shoulders tilt towards the right side of the page.

page 55: A picture of Emily's back as she sits on the bed. Her hair is tied in a ponytail. Her back is straight and her shoulders tilt towards the left side of the page.

page 62: A plate containing drops of fresh blood and bloodied tissues. Some of the blood has also stained the carpet around the plate.

page 65: The cuffs of a pair of black crutches are resting in the corner of the room. A purple light envelops the background and the crutches cast a long shadow on the wall behind them.

page 69: A black and white picture taken from the passenger seat of a moving car. The car's headlights expose the oncoming road and its cat's eyes. Ahead there is a bend in the road and the outline of a tree.

page 74: A filled bath from above. The suds in the water cling around the white ceramic edges.

page 77: A black and white X-ray of Daniel's torso, from his jaw to his hips. Visible are the plates and screws of a spinal fusion on the lower half of his back, straightening the curvature seen on page 54.

page 87: Daniel is slumped over his laptop on the sofa, unconscious due to the effects of his morphine intake. He is face-down on his laptop keyboard.

page 90: A silhouette of the mound of earth behind the garden. A full moon is in the sky with a semi-circle of a lunar halo arching over it.

page 92: Emily is laying nude on the bed, on her front. The top of the frame cuts off at her shoulders.

page 97: Emily is sat on the edge of the bed, facing away from us, towards the single window. With a towel wrapped around her, she smooths and braids her hair. The jewellery on her left wrist catches the light.